Scroll Saw Art PUZZLES

By
Tony and June Burns

FOX BOOKS
Fox Chapel Publishing Co Inc.

Publisher: Alan Giagnocavo
Project Editor: Ayleen Stellhorn
Desktop Specialist: Linda L. Eberly, Eberly Designs Inc.
Interior Photography: Tony Burns
Cover Photography: Carl Shuman, Owl Hill Studios

ISBN # 1-56523-116-3

To order your copy of this book,
please send check or money order
for $14.95 plus $2.50 shipping to:
Fox Book Orders
1970 Broad Street
East Petersburg, PA 17520

Manufactured in Korea

Acknowledgements

We would like to thank the following individuals and companies who have helped to make this book possible.
    Jim Beckerdite of RBIndustries
    Stephen Branigan of Emerald City Color Co.
    Jeremy Burns, our son
    Alan Giagnocavo of Fox Chapel Publishing Co.Inc.
    Jay Huber of Shopsmith Inc.
    Eric Jackson and Wayne Johnston of Sommerville Design.
    Steve Landry and Hanns Derke of Advanced Machinery Imports.
    Chuck Olson of Olson Blades
    Ray Seymore of SEYCO
    R. Stroulger of Hobbies (Dereham) Limited -England

Dedication

We dedicate this book to our parents, for their endless love and support made this book possible.

TABLE OF CONTENTS

We started out in 1984. Tony was teaching Industrial Arts and I was a new mom. We wanted a way to supplement our income in the summer when Tony wasn't teaching. I loved to paint and draw. So with Tony's woodworking experience and my art background, we combined our talents.

Working with wood, we designed and made everything from weather vanes to candle sconces and sold them at local shows. Tony, being as frugal as he is, could not throw away even the smallest of left-over scraps. We designed several small art puzzles utilizing these "scraps" and thus began our puzzle venture. We enjoy designing our scroll saw puzzles and being unique in our field.

Now, over fourteen years later, we are even busier. We have four children who inspire us daily with their ideas and interests, and we still enjoy exhibiting our work at shows in the northeast.

In addition is our love for the foot-powered machinery that we have collected over the years. We enjoy bringing machines to shows to demonstrate and share a bit of history and our passion for scrolling with others.

Tony and June Burns

SAFETY

1 Read and follow the manufacturers suggested operating safety guidelines provided with your machine. If you do not have these, contact the manufacturer and get them.

2 Use common sense. Think before you do it. Keep your hands away from the teeth of the blade and give yourself some room.

3 Eye, ear and respiratory protection is a must.

4 Use the guards that are provided with your saw. Note that some of the guards were removed during photography sessions for this book to clearly show scroll saw operations.

5 Eliminate all distractions. Most accidents happen when you are fatigued or distracted.

CHAPTER ONE

Choosing a Saw

We have been asked many times, "What is the best type of saw?" and "Which brand should I buy?" Our answer is, if you are going to use your saw a lot or are buying it for your business or school, stay away from starter saws. Spend the money and buy the best saw you can afford. Professional saws run better, have stronger motors, last a lifetime (with regular maintenance) and are easier to repair.

From our experience, manufacturers of good saws stand behind their saws with warranties and good service. When a saw is used extensively for many years, it will eventually need service. We have had personal experience with the companies that make the machines shown in this book. We hold their warranties and service in high regard.

Do not let anyone "talk" you into buying a saw. Always run it yourself before making a choice. Look for companies that have 30-day return policies that allow you to return a purchase if you are unhappy for any reason.

TYPES OF SCROLL SAWS

There are four basic types of scroll saws.

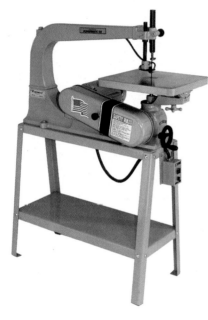

1 Rigid arm/plunger type: The upper arm of this type of saw has a spring coil that is raised or lowered by the lower (stationary) drive mechanism. Originally called a jigsaw, it was virtually the only type of scroll saw available through the late 1960's.

Atlas, Walker Turner, Delta and Powermatic were several manufacturers available in the US. Powermatic model #65 is the only model still made in this group. An antique version of this type is the Seneca Falls Challenge.

The Powermatic Model #65.

2 C-Arm: A large C-arm pivots in back where the lower center part of the "C" is connected to a motor by a bearing shaft which raises it up and down. Two examples of this are the Delta Q3 and the Delta 40-601. (Delta 40-601 is discontinued)

These saws are best known for their aggressive cutting action.

The Seneca Falls Challenge is an antique version of a rigid arm/plunger type scroll saw.

C-Arm scroll saws are best known for their aggressive cutting action. This is a Delta C-Arm (40–601).

3 Parallel Arm: On this type of saw, the upper and lower arms move parallel to each other. This is the most common saw available today. Examples are the AMI Hegner, the RBI Hawk 220 and the Shopsmith. Antique models are the Barnes #1, the Barnes #7 and the Millers Falls "Star."

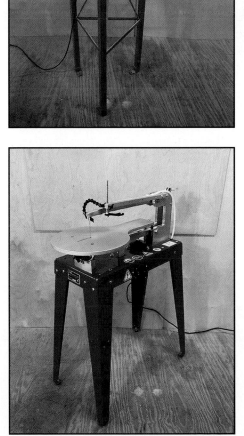

The parallel arm scroll saw is the most common type of scroll saw available today. Pictured clockwise from the right are the Hegner Multimax, the RBI Hawk 220 and the Shopsmith.

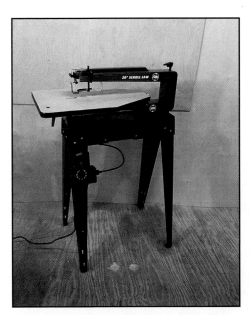

Pictured from top to bottom are three antique parallel arm scroll saws: the Barnes #1, the Millers Falls "Star" and the Barnes #7.

4 **Parallel Link:** On this saw, when the upper arm moves forward, the lower arm moves backward. This movement is converted to an "up and down" motion at the blade. The Dewalt and the Excalibur are two examples. *Note that this type of saw is known for its low vibration and smooth operation.

The Excalibur is a parallel link saw. The movement of the arms creates the up-and-down motion of the saw blade.

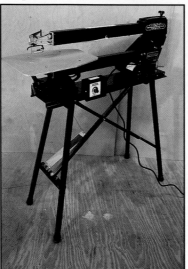

5 **New for 1999** is a saw from New Kent, Virginia, called the Eclipse. It is best described as a rigid-arm style with a flexible member. A belt connects the upper and lower chucks, which are each riding in a bearing. When the belt pulls one arm down it pushes the other arm up. The Barnes #6 is very similar in principle.

The Eclipse is the newest parallel link saw to be manufactured. The Barnes #6 (right) is an antique model scroll saw that operates on a similar principle.

6 **Variations:** A variation of the scroll saws already listed is the Beechwood, which is an odd working parallel arm saw with arm guides. The Royal Hobbies saw from the United Kingdom, circa 1904, and the Delta Scroll Boy circa 1923 both have the appearance of standard fret saws, which are raised and lowered as a whole unit by two guides with bearings. (Scotch Yoke)

The Beechwood.

The Delta Scroll Boy (above) and the Royal Hobbies (right) are two more antique models.

CHAPTER TWO

Selecting Wood

When purchasing wood for puzzle making we suggest that you buy the best grade of wood you can afford. Look for wood with a straight grain and few defects. Also avoid lumber which appears damp or heavier than usual. The following are the most common defects in wood that affect puzzle making.

Warping: It is a good idea to avoid wood that is obviously warped or twisted.

Cracks: Cracks occur in the end grain as well as along the grain of many boards. They are all hard to see. A bright light will help to make them stand out.

If a board has cracks along the grain, known as checking, it probably has more and is worthless. Even if you think you can squeeze your pattern on after the crack, there is most likely another crack there that goes unnoticed. When you see checking, there is a good chance more wood of the same lot has that same defect. It may have been cut from the same tree or improperly dried.

Knots: You can work around most knots, but many times they are visible on only one side of the board. Check both sides before laying out a pattern.

Learning about the density of each particular wood is important. This will help you to determine how strong a piece of wood is for a particular purpose. It also helps you to assess the ease of cutting and the type of blade to use.

We prefer to use silver maple, poplar, basswood and pine. These woods are readily available in our area and are relatively easy for beginners to cut. Denser woods and plywood are stronger but are harder to cut. We have also had fairly good success with 19mm solid core Baltic birch. We have a great love for oak and butternut, the latter being easier to cut. These harder woods, including Baltic birch, tend to dull blades faster, but they add fun and challenges to a great project. Your local supplier may have these or other varieties from which to choose.

CHAPTER THREE

Pattern Layout

Below are four common methods used to transfer patterns to wood. Most of the materials pictured can be found at office supply stores and catalogs. The transfer pen can be found at craft and fabric stores. The spray adhesive is available at woodworking stores.

1 Carbon paper transfer: One of the simplest ways to transfer your pattern to the wood is to use carbon paper. Lay the carbon paper carbon side down on the wood. Lay your pattern right side up on top of the carbon paper and trace over the lines with a pencil. The end result will be a carbon transfer of your pattern.

3 Iron-on transfer pen: With this neat marker you can trace a pattern onto paper (do this in reverse), and then iron the pattern onto your wood. The pattern can be transferred several times before it begins to fade.

2 Spray adhesive: Trace the pattern and spray (outdoors) the adhesive onto the back of the pattern. Place the pattern on the wood. *Note that you should remove the pattern after cutting. The longer the pattern is left on the wood, the harder it is to

4 Laminating plastic: Trace your pattern with a permanent marker onto this self-sticking clear laminate. Peel off the backing and apply the laminate to the wood. *Note that you should peel off the pattern as soon as you are done cutting your puzzle. The adhesive can break down and leave a sticky mess.

CHAPTER FOUR

Preparation for Cutting

1 Lubricating the table: I have found that lubricating the table with paste wax helps to reduce friction and allows your project to move freely on the table. We advise against using spray silicone because of possible health hazards.

2. Squaring the blade: It is a good idea to occasionally check the "squareness" of your cut. To do so, use a small two-inch engineer's square. Adjust the table to 90 degrees. This can be done on a weekly basis or as needed.

3. Checking blade thickness: A micrometer is another good investment. Being able to verify the thickness and the width of a blade helps to troubleshoot problems. It is also a good way to verify a blade size in the event the blades get mixed up.

4. Lighting: Good lighting is necessary when cutting. Incandescent light is easier on the eyes than fluorescent. If your saw does not come with a light, most manufacturers sell a light kit or a magnifying lens.

5. Anti-Vibration mat: I have found that placing one under your saw reduces vibration and operator fatigue during long sessions on the saw.

6. Elevating back of saw: By placing a 1- to 2-inch block under the rear legs of the saw, the machine is tipped forward. This reduces the stress on your neck and back. It also enables you to see your work easier.

7. Safety Gear: Three areas of safety concern are ears, eyes and respiration. A quality set of comfortable hearing protectors or ear plugs are a must if you cut for any extended period of time. For proper eye protection, quality safety glasses with side shields are necessary. If you wear tempered prescription glasses you can purchase eye shields for them.

As avid scrollers we are also concerned with the quality of the air we breathe when operating machinery. A good quality respirator is necessary to trap the fine dust and particles in the air. An example of this is the 3M model 8560/8710 (also called 8210). In addition to this, we have a permanent air filtration system (mounted on the ceiling) and a portable unit on wheels.

Lubricate the table with paste wax to help reduce friction. (Kitty Speed®, the lubricant shown in this photo, is no longer available.)

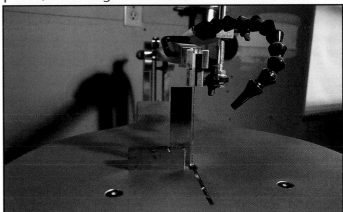

Check the "squareness" of the blade with an engineer's square.

Safety gear to protect your eyes, ears and lungs are a must.

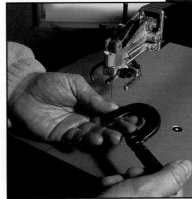

A micrometer can be used to check blade thickness.

CHAPTER FIVE

Blades

Fret saw blades (scroll saw blades) are typically made from high carbon steel that is heated, forged and drawn over many miles of rollers. This makes the steel thinner and thinner until it becomes wires of the desired thickness (dependent on gauge). The wires are then flattened. If you look closely, on most blades you may notice a slight curvature on the back of the blades. This is an indication that the blades started out as wire.

After the steel is flattened, the particular teeth style and size are ground into the steel. The blades are then heated and cooled to give them a particular temper. (It is during this process that the blade picks up its dark color,-which may appear as a dark blue. The blades are then cut to length.

Some blades are made by other methods. PGT Olson blades start out as pretempered, high-carbon steel that is double-ground to give them an ultra sharp edge. Blades can also be made by a punch or through a shearing action. They are not typically made this way today, however, because these blades are not as sharp or as uniform as ground blades.

The Olson Skip Tooth Fret Saw Blade Chart (pictured on this page) is a great place for beginner scroll sawers to learn more about blades. This is not a complete list, but it is a good place to start.

For fine cutting—3/4" (19mm) or 1" wood—we suggest that you start with a # 4 or # 5 blade. These blades will give you more detail and a smoother cut.

There is no rule that says you must use a #4 or a #5 blade. Keep in mind though that a smaller blade, such as a # 0 or # 2, will take longer to cut and may burn the wood from the extra friction. The larger blades, #9 to #12, are easier to use when you are cutting straight lines or larger radiuses, but they may not be a good choice for fine detail.

Olson® skip tooth fret saw blades

Univ. No.	Width	Thickness	TPI
2/0	.022"	.010"	28
0	.024"	.011"	25
2	.029"	.012"	20
4	.035"	.015"	15
5	.038"	.016"	12.5
6	.041"	.016"	12.5
7	.045"	.017"	11.5
9	.053"	.018"	11.5
11	.059"	.019"	9.5
12	.062"	.024"	9.5

© Olson Saw Co.

Double Tooth

Univ. No.	Width	Thickness	TPI
3	.032"	.014"	23
5	.038"	.016"	16
7	.044"	.018"	13
9	.053"	.018"	11

Reverse Tooth

Univ. No.	Width	Thickness	TPI	
5R	.038"	.016"	12.5	9 rev.
7R	.045"	.017"	11.5	8 rev.
9R	.054"	.019"	11.5	8 rev.

Crown Tooth
2-Way Cutting Action!

Univ. No.	Width	Thickness	TPI
3	.032"	.014"	16
5	.038"	.016"	16
7	.044"	.017"	11
9	.053"	.018"	6

Precision Ground (PGT)
Double Reverse Tooth

Univ. No.	Width	Thickness	TPI	
5RG	.045"	.018"	12	8 rev.
7RG	.047"	.018"	10.5	8 rev.
9RG	.049"	.018"	9	6 rev.

Extra Sharp Teeth

Precision Ground with
Reverse (PGT)

Univ. No.	Width	Thickness	TPI	
5RG	.040"	.018"	12	9 rev.
7RG	.046"	.018"	10	7 rev.
9RG	.048"	.018"	8	6 rev.

Special Reverse Teeth

Extra Sharp Teeth

Other blades that we are fond of are sold by AMI, RBIndustries and P.S. Machinery. These and other suppliers are listed in the back of this book.

Blade sizes may vary from one manufacturer to another. For example, what one manufacturer calls a # 2 blade may be extremely close to another company's #3 blade. TPI (teeth per inch) may also be measured differently from one manufacturer to the other. One company may measure teeth from tip to tip, and another may measure them from gullet to gullet. This can change the teeth count by a half of a tooth to a whole tooth.

It is important to take care of your blades. When blades are stored for long periods of time, they tend to rust. We recommend spraying them with a light coat of oil, such as WD40, to prevent rusting We know this trick works first hand, because we buy all of our blades for the year at the same time.

Blades are really the heart and soul of a saw. The finest scroll saw will not work to its full potential if you are using the wrong blade. Experimenting with different types of blades is one of the best investments you can make. This may seem costly at first, but you will be more satisfied with your results.

You'll also want to keep your blade chucks separated. One way to do this is to color code the chuck. Hegner chucks come in different sizes which can also be kept straight by color coding. Nail polish works great.

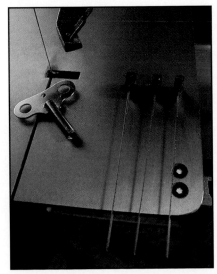

Color coding chucks with nail polish will help you to keep them separated.

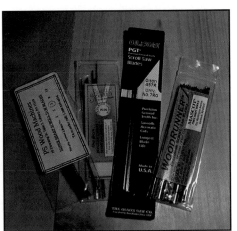

It may seem expensive at first, but trying out a number of blades is the best way to decide which blade works best for you.

CHAPTER SIX

Step-by-Step

The pansy puzzle is a challenging design for the beginner, yet satisfying enough for the experienced scroller.

Cutting

Start with a piece of wood 1/2–3/4" thick and slightly larger than the pattern (shown on page 12). We are using pine for this project, but you may want to try one of the other woods listed on page 5. The grain on the pansy project runs horizontally, but you'll want to experiment with grain direction on the other projects to see what will produce a strong finished project.

If you make a mistake while cutting out the project, your only recourse is to start over. Some projects can be saved if the cut hasn't gone too far awry. Use your best judgement, but don't be afraid to try again.

To transfer the pattern, we used laminating sheets with adhesive backing. **(Photo 1)** Use a permanent marker to trace the pattern onto the laminate. Then peel off the backing to expose the adhesive and carefully apply the laminate to the wood. You may want to try another method to transfer the pattern to the wood. (See Chapter Three for more details.)

For external cutting we recommend a # 5 skip-tooth blade. **(Photo 2)** Start at the bottom right of the puzzle to avoid leaving a visible entry cut on the completed piece. **(Photo 3)** Follow the pattern on the wood by using the blade as a pivot point. Cut to point A, rotating sharply to avoid a rounded corner. **(Photo 4)**

Cut to point B. Cut in and gently back out. **(Photo 5)** Make a sharp turn by pivoting the wood on the blade. Continue along the design to point C. **(Photo 6)** Repeat this procedure with point D.

Complete the external line of the piece by cutting to the starting point. When you reach the start, do not stop abruptly. A smooth stop will eliminate any visible entry cut. **(Photo 7)** Remove the outer scrap of wood and discard it. **(Photo 8)**

For the internal cutting of the puzzle we recommend switching to a finer blade a # 2 skip-tooth. This is a finer blade and is better for cutting finer detail.

Begin by cutting out piece # 1. **(Photo 9)**

In the center of this cut there is a sharp angle. Carefully pivot to avoid breakage. **(Photos 10 and 11)** At the exit point, slow down. This will eliminate the end grain from ripping or tearing. **(Photo 12)** Remove piece # 1 and set it aside.

Through piece # 2, cut out piece # 3. All of the little ripples in this piece will be a fun challenge (and good practice) for the beginner. **(Photo 13)** When the cut is complete remove piece # 3 and set it aside. **(Photo 14)**

At point A, cut out piece # 2 where it joins piece # 4. **(Photo 15)** On piece # 2 there are two cuts where you will enter and gently back out. Don't forget to keep the saw running when you back out of the wood. It is important to keep a good grip on the wood at all times and especially here. **(Photo 16)** When exiting the cut remember again to proceed slowly to avoid ripping the grain. Remove part # 2 and set it aside. **(Photo 17)**

Make the three detail cuts in piece # 4. Gently back out of each cut, while the machine is still running. **(Photo 18)** Assemble the puzzle. Congratulations! Your cutting is complete. If you used laminate to transfer your pattern, remove it before sanding the piece.

Sanding

We have discovered that grits from 100 to 150 work best for sanding our puzzles. A rubber mat placed under the puzzle will keep it in place. Always sand with the grain in a back-and-forth motion.

To sand our pieces, we use a sanding pad made by the 3M company. **(Photo 19)** If one is unavailable, glue a piece of rubber mat to a 3/4"x3"x5" piece of wood and use a self-sticking abrasive.

Edge sanding should be done in a downward motion, against the grain to remove any burrs. **(Photo 20)** Hold the puzzle firmly in place with one hand while you sand with the other.

Staining and Painting

The exciting designs of each art puzzle come to life when color is added. We prefer to stain our finished pieces. Staining enhances the true beauty of the grain, unlike painting which covers it up.

You can mix stains to get unique colors. The mixtures we use to get the colors for the projects in this

PANSY

book are our own "secret recipes." With a little experimenting, you can come up with some beautiful colors of your own.

Stains can be purchased from the suppliers in the back of the book.

Stain The puzzle must be taken apart carefully and each piece stained the desired color. **(Photo 21)** Staining the face of the puzzle first ensures uniform color distribution on the puzzle face. Apply the stain by dipping an absorbent cloth into the color and wiping the surface. Be sure to wipe in the direction of the grain. **(Photo 22)**. Apply stain to the end grain by using a small glue brush. **(Photo 23)** Wait

several minutes. Then wipe off any excess with a clean, dry cloth. **(Photo 24)** The pieces must be completely dry before assembling the puzzle. **(Photo 25)**

Acrylic wash Thin acrylic paint with water and apply this "wash" in the same manner as the stain. This method tends to raise the end grain slightly and is not as smooth as using a stain. **(Photo 26)**

The final details are simply applied with acrylic paints and a fine acrylic brush. **(Photos 27 and 28)**

No special finishing techniques, such as sealer, are required.

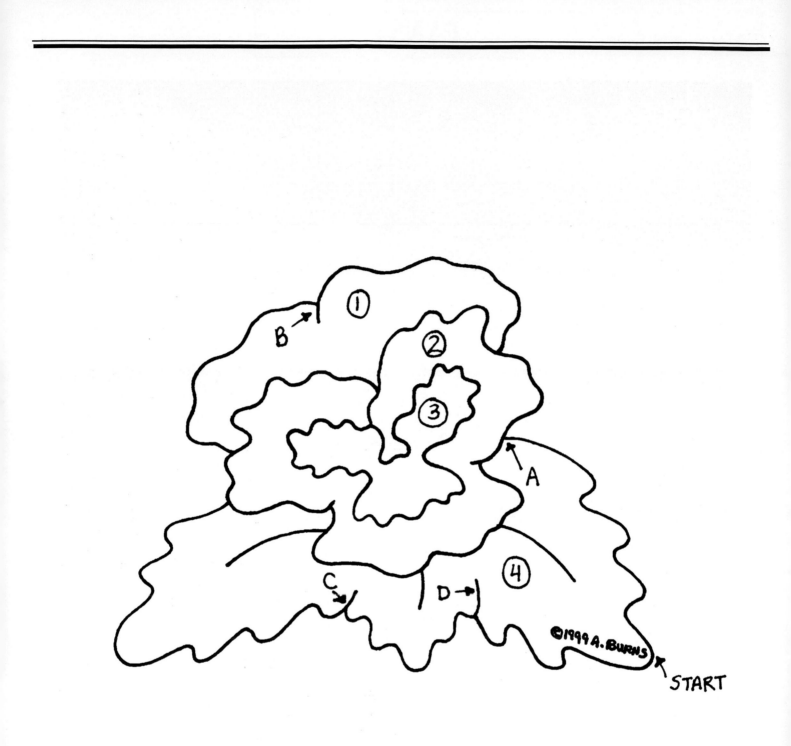

Use this pansy pattern to create the puzzle featured in the step-by-step project. You'll need a piece of wood that measures 1/2"–3/4" thick and slightly larger than the pattern. We suggest orienting the pattern on the wood so that the grain runs horizontally.

1. Transfer the pattern to the wood. We used laminating sheets for this project.

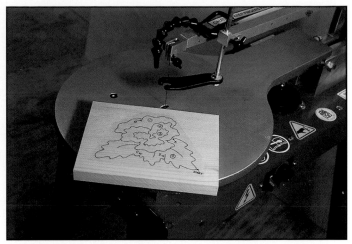

2. We recommend a #5 skip-tooth blade for the external cut on this piece.

3. Begin cutting at the bottom right of the puzzle.

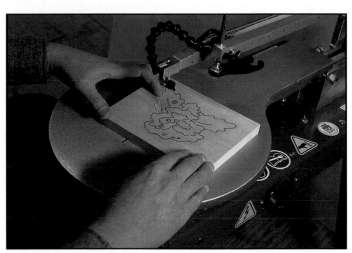

4. Cut to point A. Sharply rotating the piece will avoid a rounded corner.

5. Cut in and gently back out to point B.

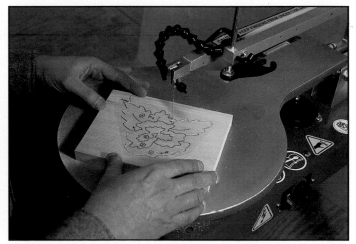

6. Pivot the wood on the blade to make a sharp turn. Continue to point C.

7. Repeat the previous step and continue to point D.

8. Carefully remove the outer scrap piece of wood and discard it.

9. Switch to a #2 skip-tooth blade to make the internal cuts.

10. The center cut is a sharp angle.

11. Carefully pivot to avoid breakage.

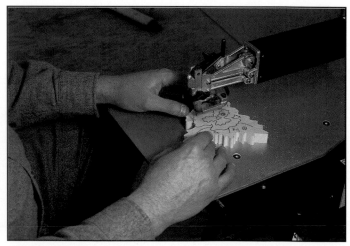

12. Slow down at the exit point to avoid ripping or tearing the end grain.

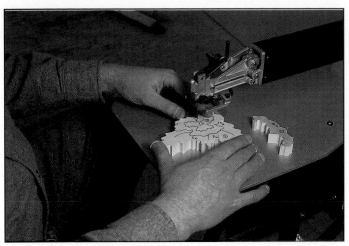

13. Cut piece #3 out of piece #2. Cutting the ripples in this piece is good practice.

14. When the ripple inside piece #2 is complete, remove piece #3 and set it aside.

15. Cut out piece #2 where it joins piece #4 at point A.

16. Enter and gently back out of the two cuts on piece #2. Be sure to keep a good grip on the puzzle.

17. Remove piece #2 and set it aside.

18. Cut the details in piece #4. Gently back out of each cut while the machine is still running.

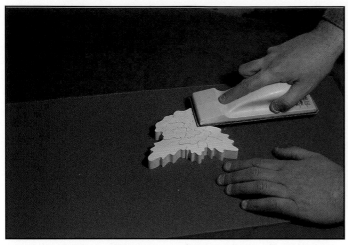

19. Using 100 or 150 grit sanding pad, sand with the grain in a back-and-forth motion.

20. Sand the edges of the puzzle with a downward motion.

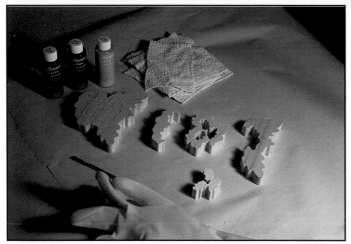

21. Take the puzzle apart and stain each piece separately.

22. Stain the face of the puzzle first. Dip a cloth in the color and wipe it on in the direction of the grain.

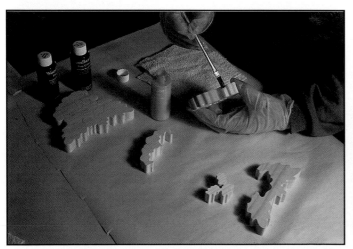

23. Apply stain to the end grain with a small glue brush.

24. Wipe off any excess stain with a clean, dry cloth.

25. Allow the pieces to dry completely before assembling the puzzle.

26. Apply final details with acrylic paints and a fine acrylic brush.

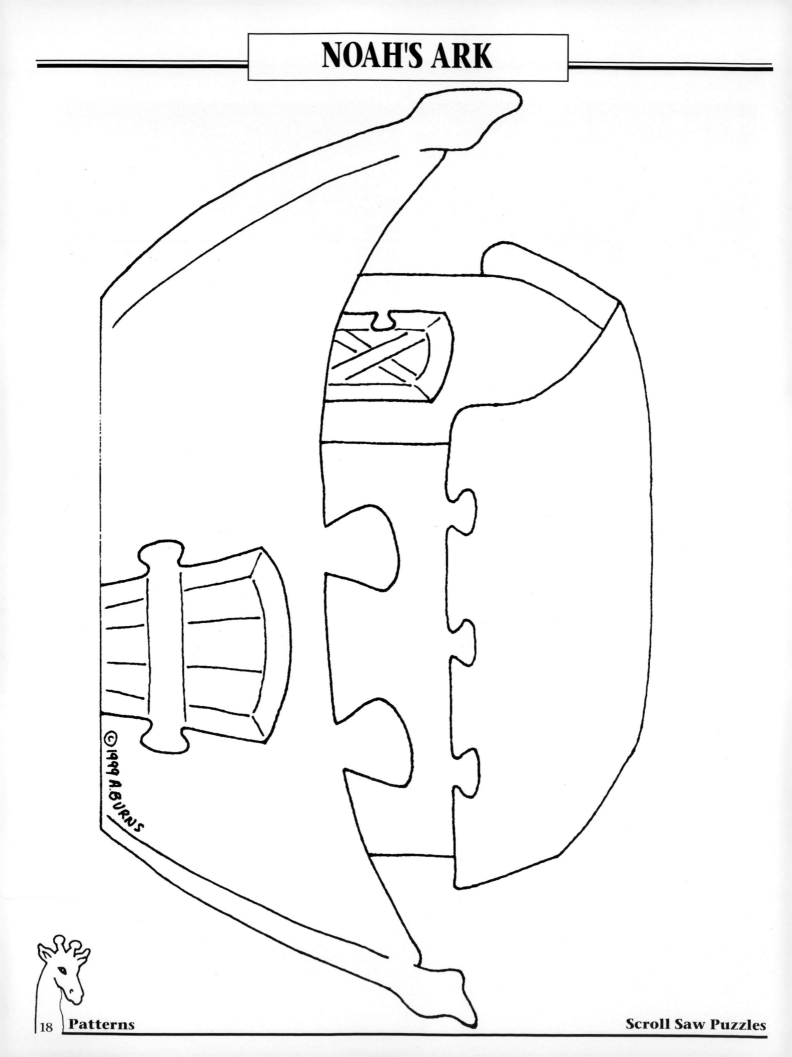

A base for the ark can be made from a ³/₄″x3″x8″ piece of wood. Make a dado lengthwise down the center of the same thickness as the ark (³/₄″). Do not dado more than ³/₈″ depth.
Noah and Wife: Noah looks great with a white beard ,too. You can also try different colors for their robes.

CYPRESS TREE

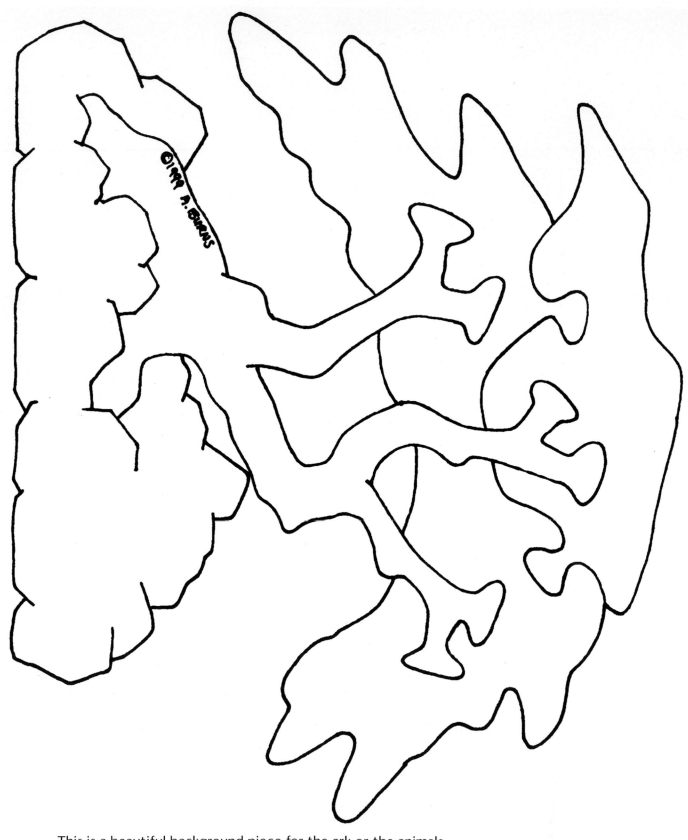

©1999 A. BURNS

This is a beautiful background piece for the ark or the animals.

KANGAROO PAIR

©1999 A. BURNS

We chose this marsupial because it is an unusual addition to the ark.

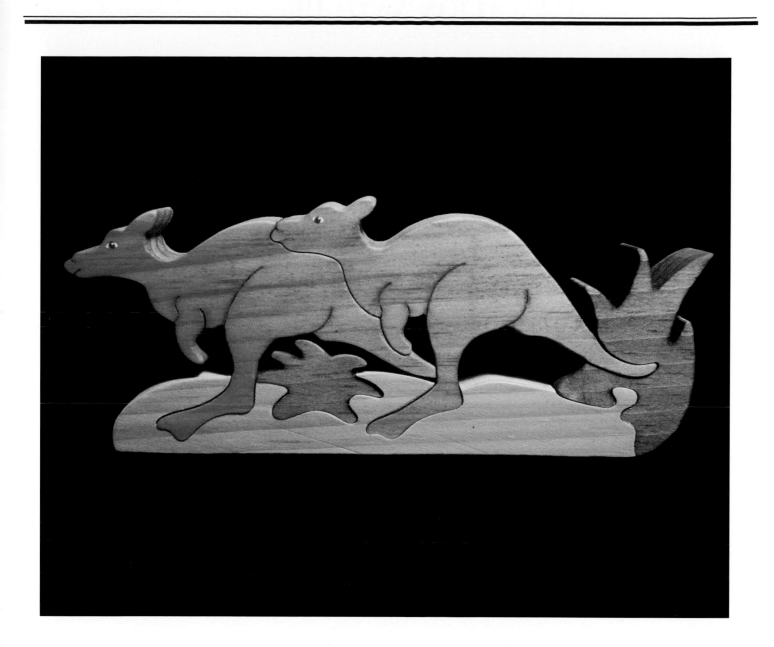

LION AND CUB

©1999 A. BURNS

What ark would be complete without the "king of beasts?"

GIRAFFES

©1999 A.BURNS

Lay out the design with the grain running vertically on this one.

TRAVELING ELEPHANTS

© 1999 A. BURNS

This seven-piece design is a fun and challenging one.

PENGUINS ON ICE

©1999 A. BURNS

The colors in this design add a nice contrast to the other animals in the ark.

DEER IN GLEN

©1999 A. BURNS

This buck is keeping a watchful eye while his doe feeds.

©1999 A. BURNS

This is a nice, simple design for beginners.

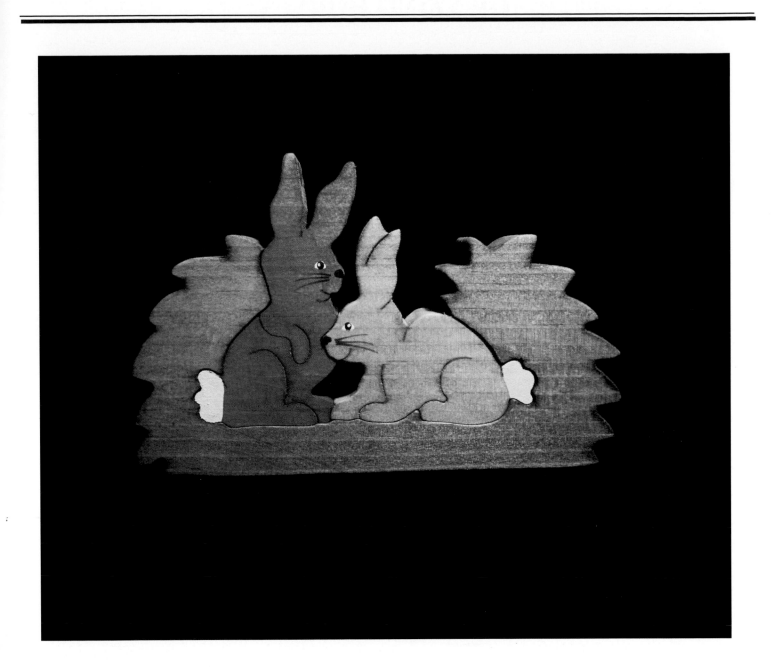

GRAZING HORSES

©1999 A.BURNS

This is a good pattern to practice cutting with and against the grain in straight lines. For this design we suggest a # 3 blade.

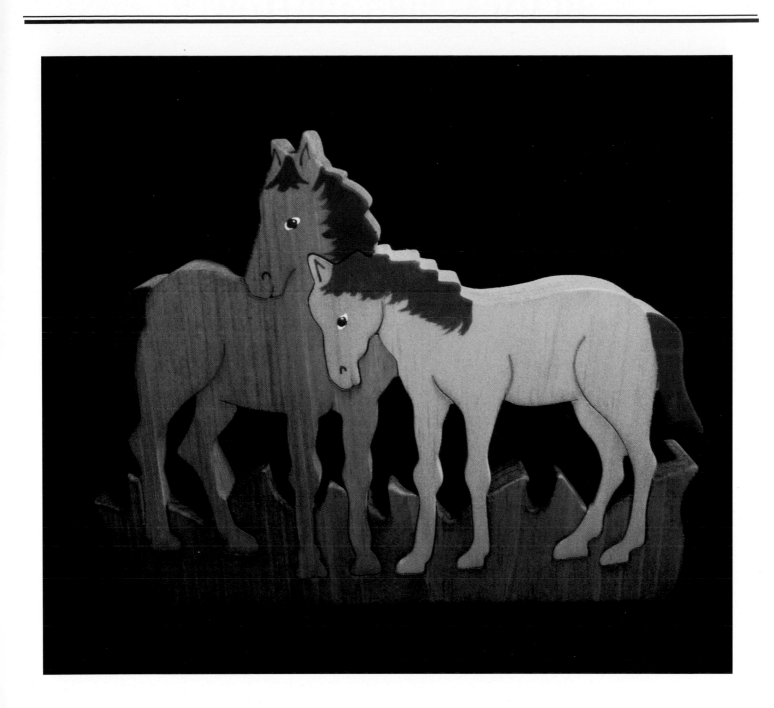

©1999 A. BURNS

The ruby-throated variety, which is depicted in the finished photo, is common in the northeast. Have fun and do a little research to discover what variety of hummingbird is common to your neck of the woods.

EAGLE IN FLIGHT

©1999 A.BURNS

This design comes alive in a three-dimensional form.

Different varieties of macaws can be achieved by changing the colors. Blue, yellow, green and red can be interchanged to create many different types.

©1999 A. BURNS

We couldn't resist doing a frog or two! This design is challenging, but don't let that stop you. Have fun with the colors. Red, blue, green, orange, yellow and black.... The possibilities are endless.

CAMELS IN THE DESERT

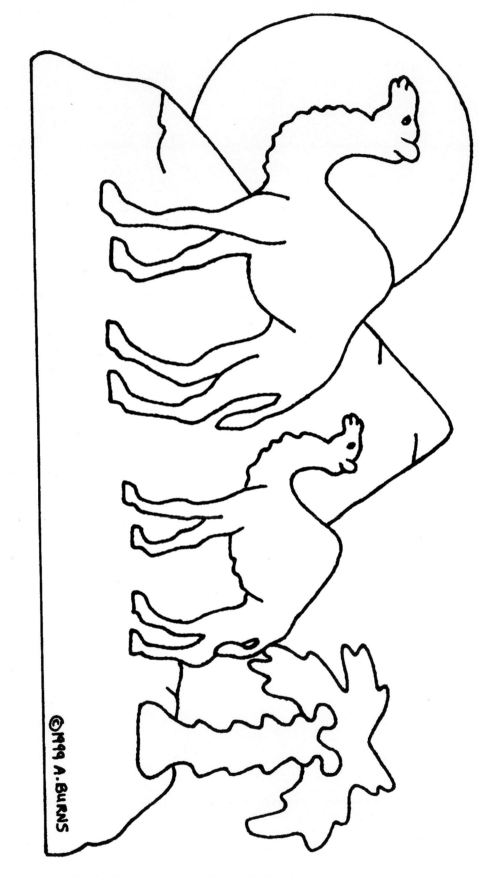

©1999 A. Burns

When laying out this design, make sure the grain is running vertical. There are some delicate areas, especially around the tails and leg. Use extra caution when cutting these.

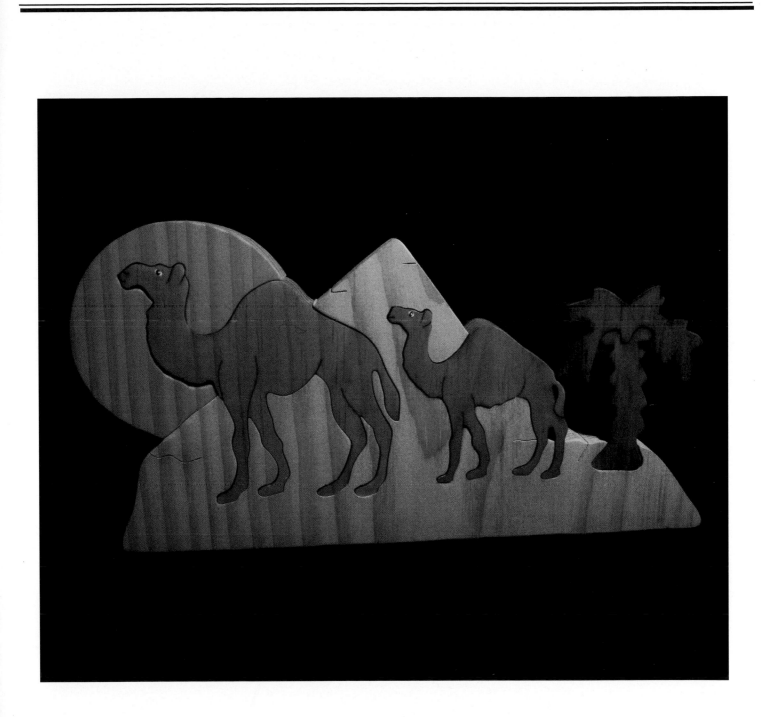

ORCA WHALES

©1999 A. BURNS

We were inspired by these "gentle giants" when we saw them while on vacation with our children.

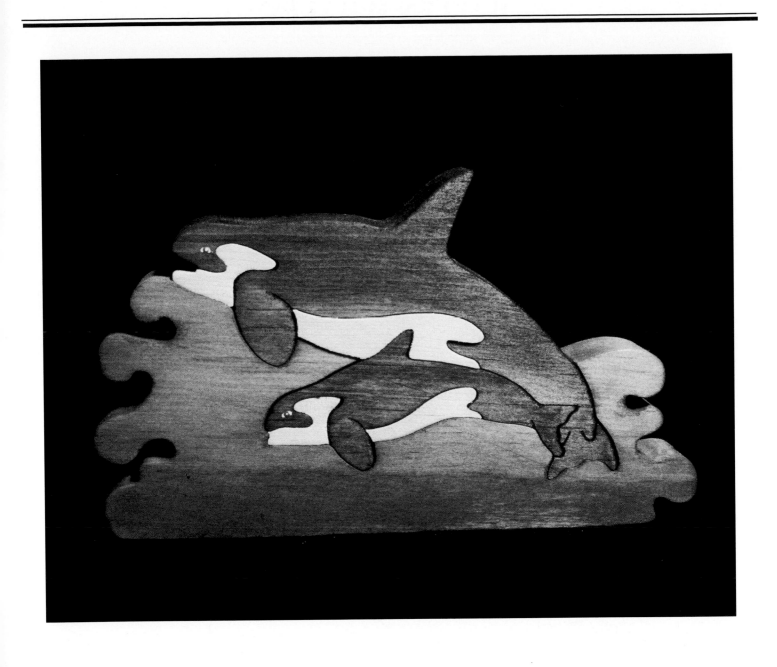

BALEEN WHALES

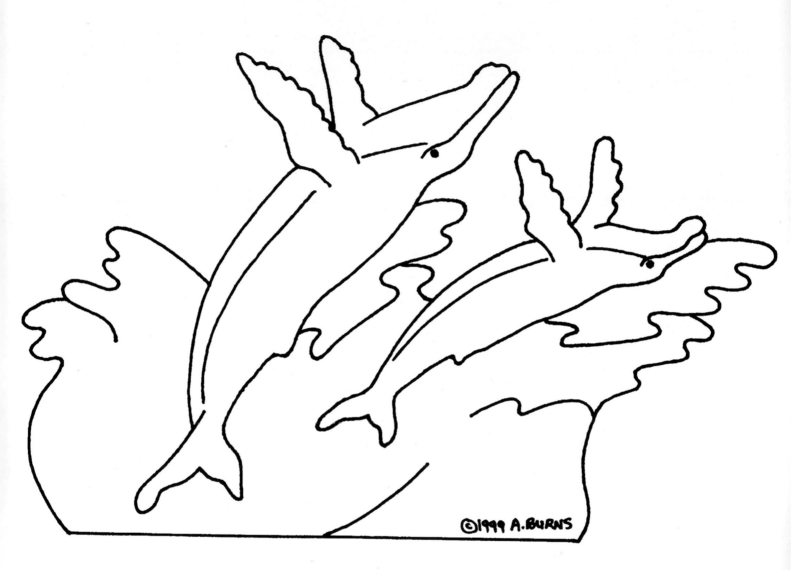

©1999 A. BURNS

These creatures are magnificent in the water.

FOX FAMILY

©1999 A. BURNS

This is a new and fun challenge, creating a layered three dimensional design.

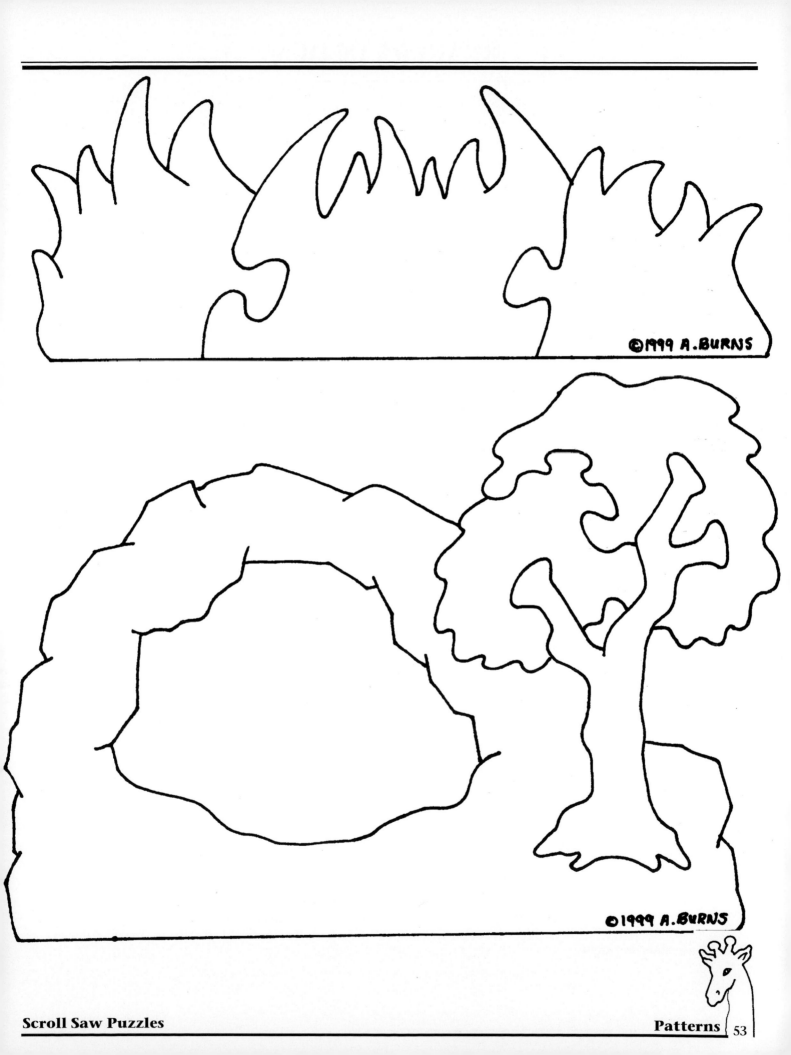

©1999 A.BURNS

©1999 A.BURNS

BEAVERS IN DEN

©1999 A. BURNS

This pattern was inspired by a visit to our local state park. To see these animals working is truly an amazing sight

CAT AND KITTENS

What little girl can resist a cat and kittens. Our daughter Anne helped us with this one. She has only one suggestion and that is to make one of the kitties gray and to name it Fluffy.

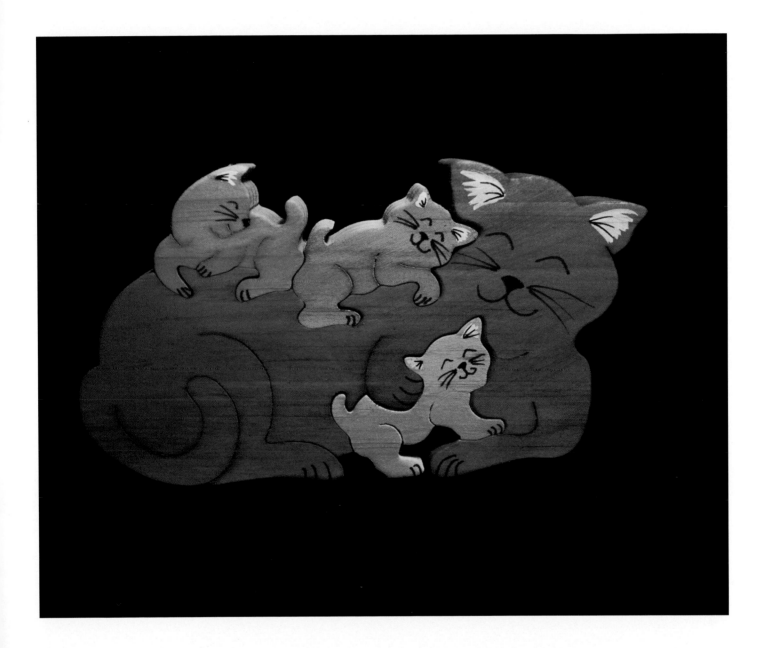

PILE OF PUPS

©1999 A. BURNS

This "pile o' pups" can be stained entirely white. Add spots and you have our daughter Annie's favorite: Dalmatians.

©1999 A. BURNS

This is another great experiment for color in design. You can change the colors of the fish to get a completely different look.

ACROBATIC CLOWNS

Make a tower of clowns by cutting a number of these clowns and stacking them on top of each other. This is our daughter Emily's favorite design.

FAIRY

©1999 A. BURNS

We designed the arm and leg on this pattern to be one piece. This can be tricky and requires an extremely fine blade, such as a # 2. It is fun to make several fairies in different colors and scatter them around your home.

Our son Jeremy helped us with this design. He enjoys drawing fantasy creatures.

©1989 A. BURNS

Wouldn't several of these make a nice grouping on a coffee table in the fall?

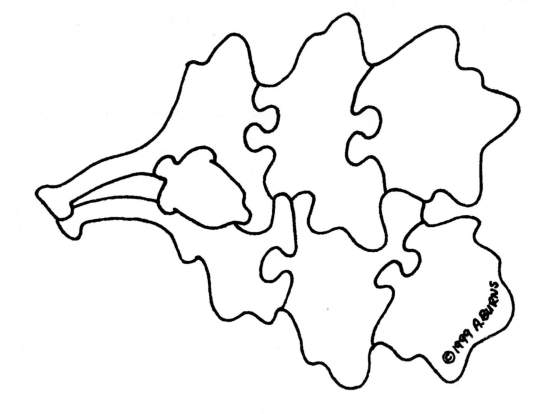

©1999 A. BURNS

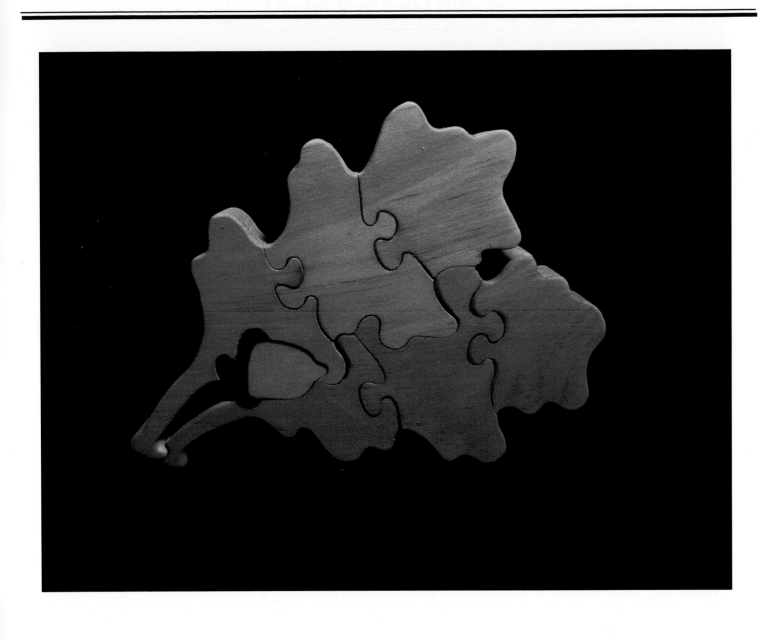

©1999 A.BURNS

We all have a guardian angel who watches over us. This makes a great get well gift.

Try a royal blue or purple for this Santa's robe as an alternative to the traditional red.

SANTA WITH STAR

This is a whimsical and fun version of Santa, just shooting across the sky on a star.

SNOWFLAKE

©1999 A. BURNS

This snowflake can be too delicate for some woods. We recommend using a solid core plywood for strength, such as 19mm Baltic birch.

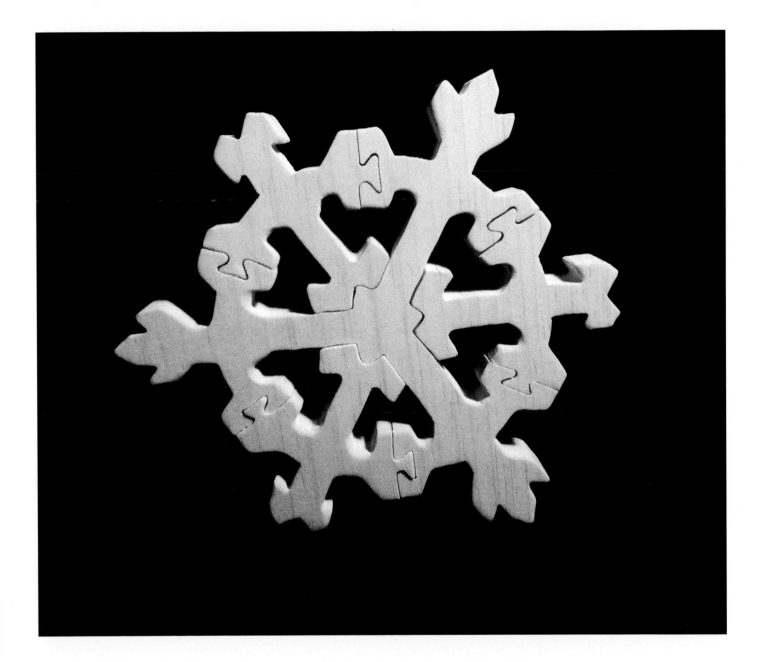

REFERENCES

Advanced Machinery
P.O. Box 312
New Castle, DE 19720
1-800-727-6553

The Art Factory
P.O.Box 701
Platteville, WI 53818
1-800-566-6394

Eclipse Scroll Saw Co.
11700 Lock Lane
New Kent, VA 23124
1-804-779-2478

Emerald City Color Co.
809 Industry Drive
Seattle, WA 98188
(206) 575-4690

Ferris Machinery,Inc.
Blue Springs, MO 64015
1-800-872-5489

Hobbies (Derehem) Limited
Derehem, Norfolk
NR19 2QZ
England

Olson Saw Co.
16 Stoney Hill Rd.
Bethel Ct. 06801

PS Machinery Inc.
10 Downing St.,Suite 3
Library, PA 15129
1-800-934-4414

RBIndustries, Inc.
1801 Vine St.
P.O.Box 369
Harrisonville,MO 64701
1-800-487-2623

S.A.W. Scroll saw Assoc. of the World
610 Daisy Lane
Round Lake Beach, IL 60073
(847) 546-1319

SEYCO
1414 Cranford Dr.
Box 472749
Garland, TX 75047
1-800-462-3353

Shopsmith, Inc.
6530 Poe Ave.
Dayton, OH 45414
In USA 1-800-543-7586
in Canada 1-800-370-3834

Sloan's Woodshop
3453 Callis Rd.
Lebanon, TN 37090
1-888-615-9663

Sommerville Design & Mfg.,Inc.
940 Brock Road
Pickering, Ontario, Canada
L1W2A1
(905) 831-4755

Wildwood Designs,Inc.
P.O. Box 676
Richland Center, WI 53581
1-800-470-9090

REQUEST

We enjoy hearing from you. Please include a
S.A.S.E. if you would like a response to your letter.
We also appreciate any information that you may
have for obtaining Foot Powered Saws for our collection. Contact us at:

Tony and June Burns
4744 Berry Road
Fredonia, New York 14063

Books by the Experts

JOHN NELSON SCROLL SAW

50 Easy Weekend Scroll Saw Projects
1-56523-108-2
$9.95
By John Nelson
50 patterns for beautiful and practical projects. Ready to use patterns.

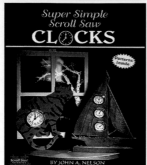

Super Simple Clocks Scroll Saw
1-56523-111-2
$9.95
By John Nelson
With your scroll saw and quartz clock movements you can easily make these 50 examples.

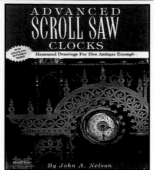

Advanced Scroll Saw Clocks
1-56523-110-4
$9.95
By John Nelson
Five amazing projects never before published. Complete, ready to use patterns.

Scroll Saw Basketweave Projects
1-56523-103-1
$9.95
By John Nelson/William Guimond
12 all-new projects for making authentic looking baskets on your scroll saw.

Horse Lovers Scroll Saw Projects
1-56523-109-0
$9.95
By John Nelson
A terrific collection of all-new projects from this popular author. Ready to use patterns.

Inspirational Scroll Saw Projects
1-56523-112-0
$9.95
By John Nelson
50 plus projects to beautifully reflect your faith.

WOODCARVING

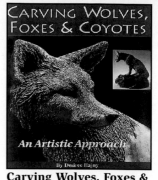

Carving Wolves, Foxes & Coyotes: *An Artistic Approach*
1-56523-098-1
$19.95
By Desiree Hajny
The most complete canine guide in color. Techniques, reference photos, anatomy charts, and patterns for foxes, wolves and coyotes.

Carving Whimsical Birds
1-56523-113-9
$12.95
By Laura Putnam Dunkle
Easy, fun and quick to carve! Good book for the beginner–uses commercial turnings.

Folk and Figure Carving
1-56523-105-8
$14.95
By Ross Oar
Explore caricature and realistic carvings in the 15 projects inside.

MISCELLANEOUS BOOKS

Making Lawn Ornaments in Wood ~ 2nd Edition
1-56523-104-X
$14.95
By Paul Meisel
New edition with 16 pages of new patterns. Only book on the subject. Includes 20 ready to use full-size patterns. Strong seller.

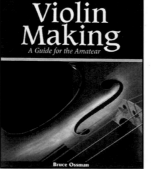

Violin Making A Guide for the Amateur
1-56523-091-4
$14.95
By Bruce Ossman
The easiest book on making violins in the home workshop. Complete set of plans included.

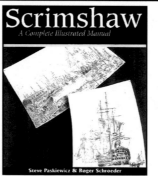

Scrimshaw: A Complete Illustrated Manual
1-56523-095-7
$14.95
By Roger Schroeder & Steve Paszkiewicz
Gorgeous full color guide for the artist and craftsperson. Step-by-step techniques and patterns.

BOOKS

More Books by the Experts

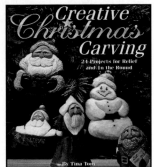

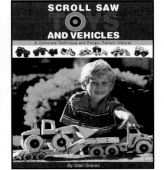

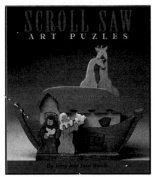

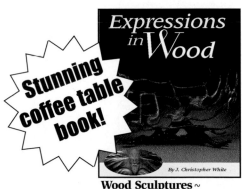

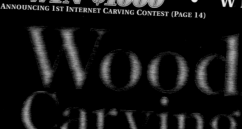